From Medicine
to Miracles

Kathryn Kuhlman

From Medicine to Miracles

DIMENSION BOOKS
BETHANY FELLOWSHIP, INC.
Minneapolis, Minnesota

From Medicine to Miracles
Kathryn Kuhlman

Library of Congress Catalog Card Number
78-67100

ISBN 0-87123-383-5

DIMENSION BOOKS
Published by Bethany Fellowship, Inc.
6820 Auto Club Road
Minneapolis, Minnesota 55438

Printed in the United States of America

Contents

Introduction . . .

Kathryn Kuhlman's earthly residence was exchanged on February 20, 1976, for a heavenly home; but before her mortal body "put on immortality," her years of service to God and others left their indelible mark upon humanity.

This manuscript was found among the "unfinished business" on her desk. We have taken the liberty to complete it, confident that it carries the same message of hope and promise that Kathryn Kuhlman declared around the world.

Yes, Kathryn Kuhlman is in the presence of Jesus, but the ministry she founded continues to be a channel of God's power, for it was built upon the never-changing Rock of Ages, Jesus Christ, and the everlasting Word of God.

It is our earnest prayer that the account of Dr. Harris' miracle will encourage you to believe God for the answer to your prayer.

The Kathryn Kuhlman Foundation
Post Office Box 3, Pittsburgh, Pa. 15230

CHAPTER ONE

Escape from the Red Chinese

My life and task as a family doctor in Pineville, Louisiana, have been to wage a constant, never-ending battle against the forces which cause sickness, pain, and death in the bodies of my friends and patients. For more than twenty-five years there has been a steady stream of men and women, rich and poor, young and old, who have waited patiently in my outer office for their turn to be examined and receive treatment. After the long office hours there have been trips to the Baptist hospital in nearby Alexandria, and, since I live in a small, southern town, house calls are expected and part of my everyday norm.

Across the years, my practice had become infinitely more difficult because my own body was wracked with constant, sometimes almost unbearable, pain. I had to practice medicine from a wheelchair, often depending on my ten-year-old son to push me up and down the hospital corridors. The proverb "physician: heal thyself" was never more applicable—nor more impossible—than it was to me.

It all began on a misty day in 1951— typical for Louisiana in December. The grey sky blended with the tops of the leafless trees as I drove down the winding highway from Alexandria to my home in Oakdale. Familiar landmarks—a white house with a green fishing skiff upended in the side yard, an open field surrounded by a sagging barbed wire fence—all tugged at the roots of my ancestry. Even though I was a physician, and had recently returned from China as a medical missionary for the Southern Baptist Convention, I was still a country boy at heart.

Dad had pastored Baptist churches in

this area for years, most of them small, all of them poor. Now he was in the Baptist hospital in Alexandria having suffered a massive heart attack. My only brother, James, who was pastoring the Beech Street Baptist Church in Texarkana, Arkansas, had come down to Alexandria that morning and called me at my office in Oakdale.

"I need to talk to you," he said. "Since I must get back home for tonight, can you meet me for lunch? We need to decide whether to contact the rest of the family and be ready to tell them if they should come on home."

That within itself would be a difficult job. Josephine was a Southern Baptist missionary in Hawaii. Virginia was at Clark Field in the Philippines with her husband in the military. Margaret, who married a Baptist preacher at Wayland College in Texas, was close at hand.

I called my wife, Ann, and told her I would skip lunch in order to drive the thirty-eight miles to Alexandria. Ann understood. Besides being married to a physician, she, too, had been raised in the home of a busy Baptist pastor in Texas. Interruptions were a part of her life.

Dad was in critical condition. He could not last much longer. His life had been rich and full, and he would soon have his crown. I spent a few minutes with him, ate a quick lunch with James, and headed back towards Oakdale. As I left the hospital the enormity of the whole situation was clear.

Dad had coronary artery occlusion with EKG evidence of considerable loss of blood supply to support the heart. It was such a large myocardial infarct that there was no hope in my mind that he would pull out of it. I knew it was far better for him to die quickly than to linger on, disabled. Nothing could be worse, I thought, than living as an invalid.

I thought of his body on the bed in the Baptist hospital, a body now frail but once so strong. I remembered all those special Sundays, year after year, when he had led the people in those little churches to give a separate offering to support the hospital. Baptist Hospital Day, we called it. Now the bread he had cast upon the water was returning.

Very few Southern Baptist pastors would ever leave the legacy my dad would leave when he died, I thought. Two of his children were foreign missionaries. Another a well-known pastor, destined to become a vice president of the Southern Baptist Convention, then president of the great Southern Baptist Foreign Mission Board, later president of the Baptist General Convention of Texas. One daughter was married to a Baptist preacher and the other a writer for the Baptist Sunday School Board. Dad had little of this world's goods, but he was going to leave behind a rich inheritance in the lives of his children.

Two ancient mules stared at me over the top strand of the barbed wire as I drove by the field. Their sad eyes followed my car down the road. Dad's pending death was just the latest in a series of events that went all the way back to our mission assignment in China. Following graduation from seminary and medical school, Ann and I had been assigned to Yangchow, Kiangsi Province by the Foreign Mission Board of the Southern Baptist Convention. Communist armies were already taking over and by 1949 we were forced to leave our practice and move to Kweilin, the only part of that vast country which had not been overrun by Mao Tse Tung's Army of Liberation. In November of that year the Communists moved into Kweilin, and I was arrested on the complaint of one of the employees in the hospital that I had been impolite to him. When I petitioned the lieutenant governor of the province to be evacuated as an American citizen, he took my passport, looked at it, and then looked back with a blank expression.

"This is nothing but paper," he said. "You don't have any country, Doctor. The United States refuses to recognize China. This forces Chairman Mao to say, 'America does not exist.' Therefore it does not exist. Your case is now being investigated. Go back to your house and wait for the completion and police report." Stateless, I was to be tried by secret Peoples' Court.

I knew I was guilty. At the hospital, a male cook had struck a female cook. I had fired him, causing him to lose face. I would be convicted. I expected a fate worse than death and started memorizing scriptures to fortify me in the Communist prison. Many of the other missionaries had families and had returned home or were entering nearby countries like Korea and Indonesia to begin work. Ann chose to stay with me in Kweilin. Only Ann and I were left behind.

Then, miraculously, one of the Chinese officials appeared and told us that I had been acquitted because of lack of evidence. The refugee train was due. We had thirty minutes to get out. Quickly we grabbed a few clothes and squeezed into a packed train for the long ride to Canton and finally on to Hong Kong. There were no windows in the train, bodies were packed tightly together, ice and snow were on the ground outside.

Suddenly one day the train jerked to a stop and everyone panicked as they scrambled out of the cars and dove into the ditches beside the tracks. Out of the clouds roared three B-26's from Formosa which strafed and bombed the train. Ann and I found a single tree to hide behind, changing sides according to the direction of the planes.

Finally we made it safely to Hong Kong, grateful to escape, but filled with concern over our many friends who were killed or imprisoned. We were forced to recognize that our heart's desire—to serve the Lord as medical missionaries in China—had been indefinitely disrupted.

CHAPTER TWO

You'll Be in Pain the Rest of Your Life

Back in the States, waiting to see what our next move should be, I accepted the offer of a local physician to help with his practice in Oakdale, a small lumber town thirty-five miles south of Alexandria. One day, I dreamed, Ann and I would return to the mission field. There were plenty of doctors to care for the sick in the States. Besides, all my years of training— Louisiana College, Southwestern Baptist Theological Seminary, L.S.U. Medical School, Yale University—all had been to prepare me for medical missions. Surely we would be home for only a short time before another assignment opened.

Now Dad was dying. Never, even when Ann and I were sheltered behind that tree while a Nationalist plane spat machine gun bullets at our feet, had I felt as alone as I did that day driving to Oakdale.

James, always the epitome of organization, was standing by in the hospital sending the messages we had agreed upon. I drove on. A heavy logging truck passed me going in the opposite direction. The muddy spray from his wheels, a mixture of mist, dirt and sawdust, blew against my windshield. My speedometer was resting on sixty and I touched the brake to slow down until my windshield cleared again.

Suddenly I felt the right wheel of the car wobbling on the sharp edge of the concrete highway. I started to yank the wheel to pull it back on the road, but it slipped off the pavement into a deep drop-off. Instantly the steering wheel was wrenched from my hands as the tire dug into the soft earth and turned sideways. I was aware of the car careening at a crazy angle and then felt it flip over, sliding on its top, down the center of the road. The top of the hardtop sedan was ripped off and I felt myself hurtling out. Then all was black.

When I regained consciousness, I was lying on the edge of the road. I had been thrown clear of the demolished car and landed on the pavement. The driver of a furniture truck had pulled me off the highway and covered me with one of his furniture blankets. I knew I was badly hurt. The mud beneath my head was squishy with blood and I could taste it in my mouth. But it wasn't my head that hurt most; it was my hip and lower back. I tried to move my leg. Nothing. The terrible thought flashed across my mind, "I'm paralyzed!" Far down the road I could see my car, upright, the hardtop sheared off and the fenders dangling in all directions.

Someone had called an ambulance. I was slipping in and out of consciousness, and when the ambulance finally arrived I kept saying, "I'm a doctor. Don't move my back when you pick me up. I'm a doctor . . . I'm a doctor . . ."

The next thing I remembered was waking up in bed in the Hargrove Hospital in Oakdale. Ann was there. So was her uncle, John Wright, pastor of the First Baptist Church of Port Arthur, Texas. I see-sawed between reality and oblivion. Each time I woke up, Ann was there, encouraging me. Several days passed. Most of the time I was in surgical shock.

"God spoke directly to me, Cliff," I remembered hearing Ann say through the fog of my semi-consciousness. "He told me you were going to be all right." In shock, there's little of any idea of death. The patient just comes and goes.

Ann believed the Bible was the Word of God. She had a strong faith in Jesus Christ as her Savior, and we had experienced many miracles while we were in China together. At the very time we left Canton on the Communist train to face our narrow escape on the Cantonese Railroad, our names had "coincidentally" appeared on the missionary prayer list used by the Woman's Missionary Union of the Southern Baptist Convention—on the very day we were spared during the bombing of our train. So Ann knew God answered prayer, not just because someone else had said it, but because we had been on the receiving end. God had told her I would live. It gave her sweet assurance.

At the end of the third week I was transferred to the Baptist hospital in Alexandria for surgery. My shoulder, wrist, and ribs were broken. I had head and back injuries. But the real damage was to my hip. The femur bone in my right thigh had been driven up through the hip socket, crumbling it. A friend of mine, a superior orthopedic surgeon, performed the seven-hour surgery. Following that, I remained in a body cast and traction for four months.

My hip socket had been destroyed by the impact of the blow. The surgeon had taken fragments of bones he could find and with the help of some metal screws, fashioned a flat hip socket. We discussed an artificial hip, but back in 1951 the method had not been perfected. By rebuilding the hip socket he expected it to fuse together—much as metal welds to metal—with arthritis. Calcium deposits

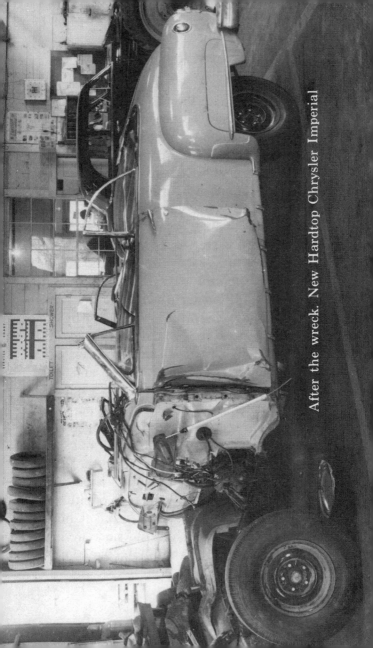

After the wreck. New Hardtop Chrysler Imperial

would grow and the bones would coalesce. The hip would be permanently stiff, and the day would probably come when I would be again candidate for surgery. But at least I could use it for a while.

"You'll be in pain for the rest of your life, Cliff," he told me. "Those boney arthritic spurs are going to rub against the sciatic nerve every time you move. You'll just have to learn to live with the pain."

After several days in the hospital in Alexandria, during which time my father slipped into eternity, I was taken by ambulance back to Oakdale. Trapped in a heavy body cast from heels to neck, all I could do was lie on my back and wait. Heavy weights were attached to a steel pin which extended through my hip and poked out the side of the cast. More weights were attached to my foot to stretch it out. I lay that way for many weeks, like a turtle in a shell, my skin rubbed raw inside the rough plaster cast. This was the type of situation in which I would be better off at home. Ann could care for me and since we lived just across from the hospital, I would never be too far away in case of an emergency. Hospital nurses volunteered their help.

I discovered that pain as a theory and pain as a reality were two different things. All during my medical practice, both in China and the States, I had stood by while people suffered. But experiencing pain myself—as a reality—was a traumatic experience, both physically and spiritually. I never dreamed how excruciating it could be, how debilitating. It was difficult to adjust to total dependence on others for my needs; then as the days dragged on into weeks my mind began to fill with plans and an eagerness to get back in stride.

My ability to commune with God, which had been so keen while I was a student at the seminary and while I was making plans to go to China, brought me great strength. Bit by bit the pain was accepted as something to live with. All I wanted to do was hasten the day which would bring the end to the agonizing intensity which seared both my body and soul like white fire.

Every movement, every vibration of the bed, every cough caused spasms of pain to race down my leg and up into my back. Each day was a struggle to fight my way back to health. The bone was fusing, and with it the arthritic spurs were growing, rasping against the sciatic nerve just as predicted. It resembled, in a small way, the pain of a dentist's drill boring into the nerve of an undeadened tooth.

At the end of four months I was cut from the body cast and my doctor fitted me with a leg and hip brace. It was a metal and leather harness that went all the way up to my waist. A special shoe was attached to it. It was designed to keep the weight off my hip. Like a giant boot, it had to be laced and unlaced every day. Gradually, however, I was able to move around the house and finally returned to my office at the hospital where I began seeing patients on a professional basis. I enjoyed the feeling of being useful again. The brace was cumbersome, but I eventually returned to my practice on a full-time basis.

Our children were still very young when Ann and I decided to move to my family home in Pineville, just across the Red River from Alexandria. I opened an office on Main Street and hung out my shingle. My orthopedic surgeon notified the Foreign Mission Board that I would never be able to return to the mission field. I would have to leave the missionary ministry to my sister Josephine, who was still with the Foreign Mission Board in Hawaii, and James who had become the pastor of the University Baptist Church in Fort Worth, Texas.

My destiny was now to practice medicine as a family physician. It was our privilege to continue active roles as members of the fine First Baptist Church of Pineville.

Since my medical professional training had been directed to preparation for Foreign Missions Medical Evangelism, the rapidly growing general practice was perhaps the closest professional life to that calling. It was no surprise to me to find that I was the same basic person facing the same medical needs universal to the human race. I was no longer hospital administrator charged with overall provision for the needs of patients, but an active member of a hospital staff with full-time attention to my individual patients.

For the first few years, I was happy to carry a reasonable load of surgery, obstetrics, office practice, and even to include house calls as part of the daily schedule of medical practice. I discovered that there were hazzards that had to be dealt with such as walking through an unlighted yard on a call. If I stepped into a hole, the wise thing to do was throw my doctor's bag in any direction and twist my body in a way that would protect the injured hip, now fused and painful to jar.

There came a day, however, when standing at the operating table through the course of a surgical procedure would leave my left leg asleep and cause increasing pain in the right. Surgery and obstetrics were dropped.

Perhaps the strangest thing in my office practice was my use of a recliner chair in the consulting room. I chose a strong Barcolounger and leaned back to elevate my legs whenever sitting to interview each patient and record the history of their illness for my files. New patients sometimes showed surprise at this unorthodox approach, but all soon became used to it. It offered an advantage when instructions were being given to patients with circulatory problems as illustration of the importance of use of the recliner to elevate the legs. In fact, this chair was not installed because of the arthritic hip, but on the theory that with the amount of torn and disorganized tissues of the hip, the great blood vessels were not exempt from involvement. Such injury might be the beginning of progressive vascular disease in which case the elevation by recliner was a form of preventive medicine.

CHAPTER THREE

What Is a Miracle?

In seeking the right atmosphere for family practice, I shied away from cold furnishings and white coat professional image. As a young doctor I had covered the walls proudly with framed diplomas, but I decided that the building of a library of books to line the walls would be proper. I chose secondhand volumes, particularly English classics in subjects related to medicine, many imported from English book sellers at surprisingly reasonable prices.

These included an old set of John Wesley's *Journal*. On reading a part of these writings one day, I found it was not the dry history of an eccentric English minister but filled with treasures of great riches which I had left neglected and covered with dust.

In one chapter he recounted a cold, rainy night when he and a friend preached and both caught colds. Wesley bounced back, his friend remained ill. Wesley went off to preach at another place and when he returned, his friend was dead. There was no heartbeat, no breathing. Wesley fell to his knees and prayed. His friend opened his eyes, recovered, and was soon preaching again at Wesley's side.

As I proceeded through the *Journal,* I had the feeling it was like reading the book of Acts. He described with simplicity how helpless he felt in the presence of insanity and knowing nothing else, dropped to his knees and prayed. He told how patients stopped screaming and cursing, fell back into a coma-like state, and then came out praising God.

I was intrigued how these people seemed to be "slain by the Spirit," that is, under the power of God, fell to the ground only to rise to their feet healed and full of praise.

All these years I had thought of Biblical happenings as part of one world and the days of my life belonging to another. To me, a healing miracle was natural in the Bible setting; whereas in today's world, God healed through use of professionals disciplined in the natural science of medicine. Yet I could not get away from the scripture, "Jesus Christ, the same yesterday, today and forever" (Heb. 13:8). If He was the same today as when He walked those roads of Galilee, laying hands on the sick, then there was hope for healing of any illness by His sovereign promise.

As a doctor I knew arthritis to be in a field all by itself. Arthritis is complex. Arthritis is mean. As life expectancy lengthens in our population, I knew arthritis would undoubtedly be the most common source of frustration and defeat of any nonfatal condition in medical practice. And I was its victim. The sharp spurs brought not only extreme pain but also mental depression. I also knew there was no known medical cure. I was doomed to its pain and crippling effects until the time for surgery.

In my practice, I had treated many arthritic patients. The debilitating pain causes them to search for any cure on earth which will ease their suffering, reaching a point where they no longer care about structural or biochemical changes. All they want is something to alleviate the pain. Some turn to all sorts of drugs, others try the chiropractors, and everyone knows about the desperate cases going to Mexico for dangerous drugs, illegal here. It makes no difference whether it is chemotherapy, hypnosis, voodoo or even some unexplainable, indefinable sovereign act of God called a miracle—when a person is being ripped by pain, all he wants is relief—from any source.

But what is a "miracle"? There is quite a range of different opinions where they are concerned. I have heard preachers say that they were at the point of collapse financially when *miraculously* just the right money unexpectedly appeared for use.

It is from our advantage of personal experience that we can testify to the common, almost routine, discussion of miracles seen and experienced on the mission field. It was by *a miracle* that I was acquitted in the Peoples' Court trial. The hospital staff had closed ranks, and with that strange and powerful matter of honor and polite Chinese custom of the courteous heart they had withstood hours of secret police gruelling without one breaking the code to please the fearsome powers over them.

Not long ago, a pastor placed a big ad in the local newspaper designating Easter as Miracle Sunday, and his Sunday school had one thousand in attendance that one day. He called that a *miracle*.

Another time a patient came to my office with the distal fourth of her finger torn off by a slammed car door. I sent the family back to the driveway to bring the separated segment and after cutting back the protruding bone, sutured it back. She left with antibiotics and a splint. Three weeks later she returned and the finger had clearly healed. She said, "God did it. It's a *miracle*." I agreed with her.

Practicing physicians are, I discovered, far more open to accept miracles than many pastors. As a rule, doctors encourage prayer for healing. Sometimes pastors prefer to avoid a clear-cut position on healing, and many seem afraid of the subject—especially miracle healings. Unfortunately, there is a very real danger of division among church members on this. Satan has used this issue to divide congregations and hinder the ministry of the church by stirring up strife and bitter division. While some have the faith to believe in the Biblical promise of divine healing for the soul, they do not believe in the Biblical promise of divine healing for the body. Limited by the boundary of natural law, some church members and leaders do not seem to understand that true miracles are founded on the unlimited, unbounded, supernatural power of the infinite God.

Against all this confusion several things are clear to me. First, a true miracle has to be a redemptive act. For it to be from God it has to bear some special relationship to God's revelation of himself through Jesus Christ. The authority for this is found in the words of the scripture, "But these are written, that ye might believe that Jesus is the Christ, the Son of God; and that believing ye might have life through his name" (John 20:31). A miracle, simply for the sake of a miracle, is not enough. It has to reveal Jesus Christ.

Second, I have no choice but to believe that miracles are for today. We arrived in China on the heels of one of the greatest revival movements in the history of the world—the Shantung Revival, which was almost a Southern Baptist exclusive. I was told by the people who were there that a genuine, sudden and unplanned spiritual awakening had shaken all of North China. Multitudes came to Jesus and healing miracles were just natural by-products which they accepted. Those who testified to these were well-educated Southern Baptist mission leaders of unquestionable integrity.

One of them, Dr. Charles Culpepper, told how his own wife had been healed of blindness. He felt that just as Wesley was sent to save England from the Great Revolution, so the Shantung Revival was sent because God knew what lay ahead as the Communists prepared to take over the Chinese churches. Dr. Culpepper told us how he came under conviction by the Holy Spirit, confessed to the Chinese congregation his sin of pride—he being the ideal combination of scholarship and spiritual endowment and was considered by all as the perfect missionary. This broke the dam and the Chinese Christians said, "He is one of us. He is a brother, not a foreigner." The Shantung Revival occurred when I was a child. It was great news to our family, but little note is made of it today. Those missionaries still living could be a source of undreamed of education and inspiration to us.

Now, merely arriving at the conclusion that God does heal today did not heal my own body. My condition was growing worse every week.

CHAPTER FOUR

The Sunday Morning God Spoke

"What are you going to do when you can't walk anymore?" my orthopedic surgeon asked me one day after I had been to his office for more x-rays and a new fitting of my hip brace.

I hedged on my answer. I had already given up surgery and obstetrics and was having to spend an increasing amount of time in a wheelchair. The prospect of not being able to walk at all, however, was more than I wanted to face.

In May something happened which brought me face to face with my doctor's predictions. Ann was in Houston visiting her sick father. I had come home early from the office, my hip throbbing with pain. All five of the children were at school and I hobbled directly to the bathroom. Hot and sweaty, I yearned for a cooling shower.

Baths were difficult. My leg and hip were completely fused so it was impossible to bend the joint. The best I could do was stand in the tub, stork-like, balancing on my stiff leg while I washed the other. But that afternoon I lost my balance. Falling backwards, with no possible way to catch myself, I managed to twist and, instead of hitting my hip on the edge of the tub, fell across it on my chest. This still meant quite a shake-up. The result was the stirring of the old pain in a new dimension. My first thought was to go on with my schedule for the few days until Ann was due home. The severe pain would not give me that choice. I entered the hospital to be placed in traction; the pain was so severe I could not sleep. Whoever said doctors are the worst patients knew what he was talking about! I did everything I could to convince the surgeon that I was all right. He finally agreed to let me go home, where I remained in bed another two weeks.

At that examination the doctor said, "Cliff, the x-rays show your hip is getting worse. The only hope is a total hip replacement."

I shook my head. "I'd have to close my office completely. It costs me more than $60,000 a year just to pay my overhead. If I don't have an income, then I'll be so deep in debt I'll never get out. I'll just keep going as long as I can make it, then schedule the surgery."

"That won't be long, I'm afraid," the doctor said.

He was right. My condition deteriorated rapidly after the fall. If I took more than fifteen steps, my leg would give way completely. The only way I could make my rounds in the hospital was to take little Cliff or ten-year-old Lance with me to push the wheelchair. They helped me get out of the car and into the chair, then rolled me into the hospital, into the elevator, and down the corridor. Outside the room I would pull myself out of the chair and stagger in to see my patients. Then back to the chair and on to the next room. When I finished my rounds my leg would be so weak that all I could do was return home and go to bed.

Finally, I gave in to the surgeon's recommendation, and he began preparations and was to let me know when he could schedule the operation. In the meantime, I struggled on, trying desperately to hold my practice and my life together.

It was almost impossible to attend church. Rest on the weekend was a necessity if I was to be able to return to my office on Monday morning.

It was on such a Sunday morning that God spoke. It wasn't audibly, nor even through a verse of scripture in the Bible. Instead, His message came through a television program featuring Kathryn Kuhlman.

I was in the living room stretched out in my recliner chair. Ann was in the kitchen, finishing Sunday breakfast so she could take the children to Sunday school. The announcer from the Monroe, Louisiana, station made the station break and suddenly there was a tall, slender woman filling the screen. "I BELIEVE IN MIRACLES," she said.

Ann was not wholly sympathetic toward women preachers. She had come from a long line of Southern Baptist ministers—most of them from Texas, which is the heartland of Baptist conservatism. But we had spent time on the mission field and had seen women function, and do a magnificent job, in places traditionally reserved for men.

I made it a regular habit to turn on KNOE-TV from Monroe Sunday morning to watch Kathryn Kuhlman. Sometimes Ann and I watched it together. We were fascinated. In the early spring Miss Kuhlman interviewed a deacon of the First Baptist Church, a police captain from Houston, who had been healed of cancer. I listened closely. He stated that he had permission to quote the M.D. Anderson Tumor Institute radiologist and had the letter to prove it. His testimony was resounding evidence that God still heals miraculously, even after the doctors have given up. As expected he mentioned that there was some disagreement expressed by another cancer specialist.

When the program was over Ann said, "Cliff, there's something to this."

"I'm sure there is," I said. "You can't ask for more dependable testimony than this from M.D. Anderson."

"Well, these people have something I don't have," Ann answered seriously. "Whatever it is, I want it."

"You're not sick," I said.

"I don't mean that," Ann said, getting up to make sure the children were ready for Sunday school. "I mean spiritually— trusting God for impossible things and seeing them come to pass. I intend to find out what it's all about. I'm desperate enough to do anything to receive the full power of God."

The subject of healing, of course, is of top importance in the life of every physician. Every day is spent studying this complex problem. Every physician I ever knew has witnessed inexplainable healings. He is apt to tell the family, this is a miracle. He may or may not see any spiritual significance, according to his own faith or prejudice.

Some of the people who were healed and were interviewed by Kathryn Kuhlman had come to her meetings expecting a miracle. Others, however, were almost dragged there by wives, husbands, or friends. It was ample evidence that God poured out His mercy on the just and the unjust and confirmed what Miss Kuhlman said as she quoted the prophet Joel, that in the last days God would pour out His Spirit upon ALL FLESH. Some of those whom Miss Kuhlman interviewed described at length the medical history and their doctor's views about their illness, its complexity and sometimes the hopelessness. Others had the audacity to say simply, "I do not understand what has happened to me. All I know is once I was sick, now I am well." The mystery grew deeper, ever more challenging.

I was intrigued by Miss Kuhlman's statement that she knew absolutely nothing

about the science of medicine. I could see
where such a flagrant admission of medical
ignorance would immediately cause some
physicians to scorn and ridicule her. Yet I
was certain Simon Peter had no knowledge
of medical science either. Nor did Paul.
One was an unlearned fisherman, the other
a genius, both Hellenist and Jewish, in
brilliant scholarship. Yet each was to per-
form many healing miracles—miracles
which, by the way, were recorded by a
physician, Dr. Luke, who penned both the
Gospel of Luke and the book of Acts. In
fact, I could understand how the lack of
medical facilities, as John Wesley found,
made more dramatic each healing as only
divinely possible—the power of the Holy
Spirit of God. Miss Kuhlman did not
"know," as we of the medical profession
know, that some diseases are "incurable."
Of course, viewed from the platform of
medical science some diseases are indeed
incurable. But seen as God sees, from the
platform of heaven, nothing is impossible.
Deep inside I was grateful for the fact that
Kathryn Kuhlman was not a medical scien-

tist. Instead of studying about things incurable, she fastened her eyes on the eternal promises of the God of the impossible.

Leonard Sanderson, Director of Evangelism for the Louisiana Baptist Convention, was directing the spring revival in our church. I attended some services and missed some. Ann and the boys managed to go every night.

I was in bed when Ann came home from the revival Wednesday night. She came straight to the bedroom.

"I'm afraid I made a fool of myself tonight," she said.

I looked up. "What do you mean?" I asked.

She sat down on the end of the bed. "The church was full and we were near the front. The singer asked for testimonies and nobody said a word. Suddenly I was on my feet compelled to speak. I told them 'I cannot sit here and not say something for my Lord. I want to tell you He is real and I am looking for a miracle in our family.' "

"What kind of miracle did you have in mind?" I asked.

"I don't know," Ann said. "I didn't even mean to say it. I was just upset that nobody would get up and testify for the Lord. But when I got to my feet, that came out."

Ann turned and looked straight at me. "I talked to the boys in the car on the way home," she said. "I think God made me say that for a particular reason." She paused, caught her breath, and continued. "Cliff, we are going to ask God to heal you."

CHAPTER FIVE

The Inquiring Mind of a Doctor

I looked up at the doorway of the bedroom. The boys were standing there. They had been taking turns massaging my leg with an electric massager. This time, however, they were there for a different purpose. Without saying a word they all knelt alongside the bed. One after another they prayed, asking God to heal my body. I remembered the words of the prophet Jeremiah, "Is there no balm in Gilead; is there no physician there?"

Then an old hymn we used to sing in Dad's country church came to mind:

The great physician now is near,
The sympathizing Jesus;
He speaks the drooping heart to cheer,
Oh, hear the voice of Jesus.
Sweetest note in seraph song,
Sweetest name on mortal tongue;
Sweetest carol ever sung,
Jesus, blessed Jesus!

He is the balm in Gilead. He is the great physician. By His stripes we are healed. I felt nothing, but deep inside there was a peace. He was more than healer. He was Lord. I drifted off to sleep, remembering the words of another scripture passage: "My times are in your hands."

A week later, Brooks came bouncing into my bedroom.

"Guess what, Dad," Brooks said. "Kathryn Kuhlman is going to be in Monroe next week. I heard it on TV this morning."

"When is the meeting?" I asked.

"May 17," Brooks bubbled excitedly. "A Wednesday night."

Lance, our ten-year-old son, who had been standing outside the bedroom door, pushed past his mother. "Daddy, Mom and I have been praying. She asked me what I would like you to do with me after you're healed. I told her I'd like for you to take me to a ball game. You've never been able to take me to a ball game. You're always too sick."

The room got quiet. Little Lance just stood there, looking at me. I lay back on the bed and stared at the ceiling. *Sometime, Cliff Harris, you're going to have to give an answer to this. You say you believe in a God of miracles. Now your own son is calling you to lead him in this profession of faith.*

I propped myself up on the pillow. "We'll see," I said.

A smile was spreading across Lance's face. "Not only a ball game, Dad, but maybe you'd take me fishing too. I've never been fishing. Not in all my life."

There was no chartered bus from Pineville for the service, yet somehow it seemed right we should go to Monroe. To this day I cannot explain how God arranged for the office lull to spring me free. As soon as the boys arrived from school that Wednesday afternoon, we were ready to start the drive to Monroe.

It is ninety miles from Pineville to Monroe. I knew it was going to be a difficult ride. I sat in the back seat with Marshall while Lance rode in the front with his mother. My wheelchair was in the trunk. I was wearing the right leg brace.

"I'm just going to study the situation," I told Ann as we pulled away from the house. "This is a great chance for a doctor to learn." Since I planned to have hip surgery, it did not occur to me that I even needed a miracle.

The meeting was to begin at 7:00 p.m. and we arrived in Monroe a little after 6:00. Every parking space within four blocks of the Civic Auditorium was taken. We'll never make it, I thought. I knew it was impossible for me to walk that distance and it would be almost as difficult if the boys had to push me in the chair.

Ann, however, drove right to the front door. The auditorium was obviously filled, the doors shut, and those who could not get in had left. The only lights were those in the distant parking lot. A worker with a lapel badge was standing near the curb.

He stepped to the car as we stopped. "I am a wheelchair patient," I said. "Is there any room left in that section?"

The man bent over and peered through the window into the back seat. "Yes, we can take you to the wheelchair section," he said. "But only one person can go in with you. The auditorium is packed and there are no other seats."

As we unloaded the wheelchair, I turned to Lance and suggested that he push me in. He had so faithfully and without complaint pushed me on rounds in the hospital.

"Where can I park?" Ann asked.

The man shrugged his shoulders. "Any place you can find, lady," he said.

"There's a place up there," Marshall said excitedly, pointing just three cars ahead. "Right in front of the auditorium."

Lance wheeled me through the side door, down a long ramp and into a section reserved for wheelchairs near the back of the big auditorium. Moments later I saw Ann and Marshall coming in and taking seats on the concrete steps just a few feet behind us. I don't know how they managed to get in or how they found seats. Like the parking space, they just seemed to appear at the right time.

The auditorium was like a huge indoor stadium with a stage on one end and people sitting in tiers all around. A tremendous choir had gathered at the far end behind the platform and the director was putting them through the final stages of rehearsal. The assembly had something of a carnival atmosphere, except instead of being raucous and rude, the people were warm and friendly, exhibiting love, joy, and happiness. Seemingly there were no strangers. There was an air of expectancy.

I was deeply touched by the number of sick people around me. Across the aisle was a beautiful young girl on a stretcher. A portable respirator provided the air she needed to breathe. As I talked to the sick about me, asking the nature of their illnesses, who had treated them, and what they expected here, I could not miss the restless moving of the small children near me—some of them in wheelchairs. It was a long wait for the service to begin, so I sent Lance out to the lobby where they were selling refreshments. He came back with ice cream and popcorn for the children.

Miracles I might or might not find, but I was an expert at making children happy. I felt at home and very soon I knew most of their names. I had arrived at the meeting with the inquiring mind of a doctor and I enjoyed sitting there in my wheelchair seeing how many correct diagnoses I could make of those about me. I knew what Ann was probably thinking. She would be praying for the service and for the patients. It did not occur to me that I might be one of the patients.

CHAPTER SIX

Claims of Healing

The meeting started and Kathryn Kuhlman appeared on the platform. There was much singing, both by the choir and the congregation. The music was inspiring—even the sick people in the wheelchairs were joining in, many of them lifting their hands as they sang. My eyes were roving around the auditorium, particularly the wheelchair section, taking it in.

Several people were called to the platform to testify, but I paid scant attention. Like a spectator at a circus, I was more impressed by what was happening around me than by what was taking place on the platform. I did pray, silently, for the tragically ill near me.

56

Next was the sermon and I couldn't help but be impressed with what Miss Kuhlman was saying. I was delighted to find her theology agreed with mine. She majored on the Lordship of Jesus Christ, the divine inspiration of the Bible, the atoning power of the blood, and the second coming of the Lord. It was all familiar ground to me. Her theme was lifting up the person of Jesus Christ and emphasizing the power of the Holy Spirit. I have never heard anyone give quite the same sound when speaking the name of Jesus and it carried weight. She made it clear that she disclaimed any credit for the miracles she expected to follow.

Kathryn Kuhlman suddenly pointed in the direction of the choir behind her. "Someone is being healed of asthma," she said. "Come to the platform and claim your healing."

Now was the time to be alert and investigative. Was there an instantaneous healing by supernatural power? Such power can come from only one of two sources—God the Father or Satan. Many times she rebuked Satan, but constantly was lifting the name of Jesus. So, the source of her knowledge of the healing could only be the Holy Spirit.

Miss Kuhlman called out again, "Someone is being healed of asthma." A choir member responded, but asthma is so complex that even as that one came forward and said he had been healed, there were medical gaps which needed clarification.

The next healing she called out was arthritis. Here again was something not easily measured scientifically. Arthritis is mean and unpredictable. I have seen remissions lasting years with no complaint. Medical research is also here revealing revolutionary concepts of causes and course of this common disabling and painful illness. Before a doctor would believe that the power to heal arthritis was present, something more than a simple claim was needed.

The claims of healing continued. I tried to measure each patient and his claim from the vantage point of common sense. Of course there was no way to validate these claims from where my wheelchair was located. To support or doubt these claims was not my problem.

Suddenly, another phenomenon caught my attention. I had found it told again and again in the Bible, and had read about it in histories of great religious awakenings, including biographies of great preachers like Finney. But I had never had the privilege of witnessing the sight. When Kathryn Kuhlman prayed for people after their testimony, they fell backwards to the floor. There were volunteers on the platform, acting as if they expected this and were in position to catch the person and lower him to a recumbent position on the floor. Any doctor doing such a thing could expect a million dollar suit based on claim of back injury, and each fall usually came as a complete surprise to the one who fell.

My mind flashed back to Wesley's *Journal*. A traveller passing the open meeting idly stopped and was smitten to the ground. A Quaker who admonished bystanders against these strange scenes was himself struck down as by an unseen hand.

To a student of theology, the most famous such experience is the Damascus Road experience of Saul of Tarsus. In many unexpected places in the Bible may be found incidents of people falling backward in relation to God's power. I believe the Bible is the authoritative inspired Word of God. I was unfamiliar with the term I heard that night, "slain in the Spirit," but seeing it happen, I could in no way think of it as heresy, unnatural or staged.

I listened to Kathryn Kuhlman's theology. It most impressed me as an outpouring of God's love and hope. She moved freely and gracefully from person to person with no effort to impress them.

From my lifetime standpoint of thinking, perhaps the most unexpected thing was the presence of priests and nuns seated on the front row on the platform. They were there to be prayed for that they might be "filled with the Spirit." Most fell to the floor gracefully. My background as a Southern Baptist, including many discussions with Catholics about doctrine or dogma, made this seem indeed strange to me. Were these priests actually looking to a Protestant woman for the "baptism"? I had no answer except to assume that both priests and nuns here were looking beyond Kathryn Kuhlman to the Father—to the Heavenly Father.

Her joy, her wit, her enthusiasm, her natural manner of avoiding being critical or negative in expression revealed a sound Biblical position of proclaiming God's love, saving grace and power.

There was a small man in a wheelchair. I could not even speculate on his diagnosis, because all that was said was that he could not stand and had no feeling in his lower extremities. He walked uncertainly at first. Then he bent over and pulled up his trousers so he could feel his legs to make sure they were real. He provided some comic relief when he told Miss Kuhlman he was a former tap dancer and asked permission to try out his "new legs" and tap dance on the stage.

"Be my guest," Miss Kuhlman

chuckled. To the delight of the audience the man tapped all the way across the stage. When he returned to the microphone, Miss Kuhlman reached out to pray for him, but before she touched him he was lying on his back. It was a delightful spectacle.

There was a tall, slender girl in her twenties with long, yellow hair who came on the platform with a friend. She had just recently been given the final diagnosis of glaucoma with the advice to prepare for a life of total blindness, for there is no cure. Her friend, who had led her into the auditorium, confirmed this. Some time during the service, she received her sight and could now see well enough to count Miss Kuhlman's upraised fingers, even when she backed off across the stage. The audience burst into applause and rose to their feet to sing "How Great Thou Art." She confessed that she was not a church-goer. "I have never thought that God was real," she said. "But now I will never doubt that He *IS* real."

One man, a Southern Baptist, was healed of deafness in one ear. As he left the stage Miss Kuhlman said something which deeply impressed me. "Baptists are strong believers of the Bible, but many do not fully realize the potential power that is theirs. One day they will shake the world for God when they catch a glimpse of the power of the Person of the Holy Spirit."

CHAPTER SEVEN

The Word Impossible Is Not in God's Vocabulary!

I was trying to sort all this out in my mind when I felt a tap on my shoulder. I looked around. It was Ann.

"My thumb has been healed," she said.

For several years, following an accident in which Ann had been struck by a truck while she was riding a bicycle, her thumb had been numb, without feeling. "I was sitting back there and suddenly felt a strange heat in my thumb," she said. "Now I can move it. All the sensations have returned. I think we should go to the front," she continued.

"Fine, let's go," I replied.

We started down the aisle, with Ann pushing the wheelchair and me saying, "Excuse me, excuse me, excuse me," to the people who blocked our way. Halfway to the front, those standing in the aisles trying to see better had jammed so tightly in the space that Ann said, "It's hopeless. We can never get through this."

My reply was, "We started because we felt led. We will not be discouraged. We will make it."

Ann pushed on and we slowly made our way through the crowd to the front near the steps leading to the platform. I heard the man in front of us talking to a lady worker.

"Have you had a healing?" the worker asked gently.

"That's what I've come for," the man answered. "My spine is twisted and I want Miss Kuhlman to lay hands on me and pray."

"I'm sorry," the worker said kindly, "Miss Kuhlman is not a healer. She seldom lays her hands on the sick. She simply reports what God is doing in the meeting.

Please return to your seat and keep on praying. Surely God is not through with you yet."

Then the worker turned to us.

"My thumb has been healed," Ann said emotionally, "but I'm more concerned about my husband in this wheelchair."

"Have you had a healing?" she asked me.

"I don't think so," I said honestly.

"How would you ever know, sitting there in your wheelchair in a brace?" Ann was saying. "Try to get up."

As a medical doctor I do not respond to orders from other people. Ann is the exception to this rule. I put my hands against the arms of the chair and pushed upward. As I stood erect Ann bent over to unsnap the heel brace.

"Oh, look, Cliff," she said. "See how I can use my thumb."

But I was not thinking about her thumb. "Let's get this brace off," I said, totally unaware of the thousands of eyes which were focused on us as we stirred around at the base of the platform.

The worker reached out and touched my arm. Then pointing to Lance who was standing beside us, she said, "Why don't you go with your father to the rest room downstairs. Help him take off his brace." Turning back to Ann she continued, "You stand right here and pray. When he gets back I'll come and check him."

I walked through the side door and down the concrete steps. Once inside the men's rest room I slipped off the brace and tested the hip. There was no pain.

I handed Lance the brace as I started upstairs. I had counted the steps on the way down. Twenty-five. The last time I had tried to walk upstairs, I couldn't make it. But now I was able to climb them, though not as normally as I could have done twenty-five years before, but with seemingly little effort. I didn't have to hold on to the handrail or drag my leg. The way my legs were functioning was amazing.

When I reached the top of the stairs, Ann and the volunteer were waiting. "How is it?" they asked.

I had been a doctor too long to make spot diagnoses—especially in areas I could not positively confirm. I knew there was strong evidence, but it was all subjective. Could this be termed healing? Because I was the patient, that must wait, at least until I had been examined. Arthritic patients often have remissions. And I assumed that under great emotional stress the symptoms of pain could leave temporarily. But I was not under emotional stress. And certainly this was too dramatic and instantaneous to be classified as a remission. Yet I knew until I was examined and until this "healing" stood the test of time, I could not give a positive diagnosis. Therefore all I could say honestly was, "Well, I have no pain. That's all I can say."

"Why don't you test it?" the worker said.

I had found, by climbing the stairs, that I could put weight on the hip without pain. But the ultimate test would be to jump on it. I said, "Okay, here goes." I started jogging down the open space between the seats. Behind me I could hear Lance's penetrating voice. "I've never seen my daddy run before!"

I turned and jogged back, deliberately

jarring my hip with each step. The pain was gone.

I was now having a new kind of problem. What should I say? I wanted to believe I was healed, but I was still the patient and too much of a scientist to claim more than I could prove. I needed my doctor.

"I can't say I'm healed," I said with determination. "All I can say is I don't have any pain."

The worker motioned for Lance to place the brace on the platform. "Let's go up on the stage," she said. "I'm sure Miss Kuhlman wants to know what has happened to you."

Most members of the medical profession shy away from any sensational display. Besides, at that time there was absolutely no means to verify any kind of healing. All I could say with certainty was that the pain had disappeared and I was able to walk. We moved towards the steps leading to the platform. Jimmie McDonald, Miss Kuhlman's soloist, had me by the arm and was propelling me toward the center of the stage.

"What's this?" Miss Kuhlman asked.

"This is Dr. Harris, a medical doctor from Pineville," Jimmie said. "He came to the meeting in a wheelchair but has been healed."

"What is a medical doctor doing up here?" was her opening comment. I tried to protest but the roar of the crowd was too great. "Say, it sounds like you have some friends out there," Miss Kuhlman laughed.

I hadn't intended to get into all this. Here I was on the platform in front of all these people, forced to testify to something I myself was unwilling to medically confirm.

I tried, once again, to make it clear.

"I can't say that I am healed," I protested. "All I can say is I have no pain."

"Well, have you been able to bend your leg at the hip?" Miss Kuhlman asked.

"Not in twenty years," I answered.

"Try it now," she said.

I obeyed. To my amazement I was able to squat all the way to the floor. I did it several times, up and down.

"Impossible!" I said. "It is fused together with arthritis. The joint has been frozen with arthritic spurs."

"Impossible?" Miss Kuhlman laughed. "Doctor, don't you know the word *impossible* is not in God's vocabulary?"

"But I still cannot say for a certainty I am medically healed," I said. I wanted to get off the platform, but Miss Kuhlman was holding my arm while she talked.

"Let's see you run across this stage," Miss Kuhlman said.

I obeyed again jogging the width of the stage, allowing my right foot to hit the floor each time with a heel-jarring impact. There was no pain. The crowd applauded wildly and I was left in the untenable position of a man of science who was trapped by his knowledge of science.

Seeing no way to escape, I stood talking to Miss Kuhlman, trying to be polite, but having to choose my words carefully. I said, "If a patient came to me presenting the picture I present tonight, I would have to say nothing of medical significance has happened." I could not profess or accept a healing that was not real. By now I was wishing I could claim a healing.

CHAPTER EIGHT

Let's Put This to the Test

Relieved and happy to have closed the subject, I was practically in the act of leaving, convinced that Miss Kuhlman was a fine, sincere, orthodox religious lady who was somehow causing strong psychosomatic experiences in certain impressionable people. There was no doubt in my mind about her commitment to God and her strong desire to help these people. Nor was there any doubt that the pain had left my hip. But at that point I knew I should not connect the two and felt that from a medical standpoint it would be better to gloss over the matter and just return to my seat.

As I turned to leave, however, Miss Kuhlman reached her hand toward me and started to pray. I heard only two words: "Dear Jesus," and I felt myself falling backward. I had noted that the volunteer helpers had drawn away. Nobody was around us at the time. It happened so fast that even the men who would ordinarily catch the people as they fell could not get to me. Unable to stop myself or cushion the fall, I crashed backward to the floor like a six-foot timber—hitting with a crunch on my hip shoulder and head.

I felt no heat, electricity, fear, or alarm. Most important, I felt no pain. It was as though I had stepped out of my body and let it fall, landing on a soft, fleecy, cumulus cloud. At the same time I felt an inexpressible peace filling my whole being. I do recall being puzzled. I did not feel contact with the floor. Yet how could my hip take such a blow without feeling the excruciating, stabbing pain I would expect? This peace and relaxed feeling stayed with me as I got to my feet.

Miss Kuhlman was saying, "Now what

do you say, Doctor?"

My reply was something like, "I was knocked down but you did not do it."

"That is exactly right," was her answer.

Marshall and Lance were waiting for us at the bottom of the steps. "Your face, Daddy," Marshall said. "It's changed. It's full of color."

As we returned to our seats in the rear of the auditorium I heard Miss Kuhlman say, "There goes a Southern Baptist who'll never be the same again." Then she repeated something she had said earlier, but in a different way this time. "When Southern Baptists believe what they confess, they are going to set the world on fire." Her words had a prophetic ring.

I sat on the concrete bleacher steps the rest of the service, watching that slim, wisp of a woman moving about the platform under the anointing of the Holy Spirit. I was yet to find how dramatically that night was to change my life. How strange are the ways of God!

Jesus was accused of working the works of Satan, not of God. Pentecost was total confusion and the disciples were referred to by the bystanders as a crowd of drunks. Paul was called "mad" and had a talent for causing riots.

John Wesley left Savannah on foot by night, a fugitive. Later, as the influence of his society grew, he was called a fanatic and a disgrace to the Church of England because he preached to the poor in open fields.

I always thought Charles Spurgeon was such a successful giant as a preacher, that he was universally admired and untouched by attacks. Yet he said, "Scarcely a day rolls over my head in which the most villainous abuse, the most fearful slander is not uttered against me both privately and by the public press. Every engine is employed to put down God's minister. Every lie that can be invented is hurled at me. I have seen men bite their lips and grind their teeth in rage when I have preached on the sovereignty of God."

Today's Christian leaders are criticized, mocked and ridiculed. Even among our Southern Baptist ranks, those who dare to explore new truths are unavoidably the center of controversy. Scholarly Dr. T. B. Maston, my former teacher and professor of Christian Ethics at Southwestern Baptist Theological Seminary in Ft. Worth, Texas, had suffered the harshest vilification and denouncements. Some in our own denomination had called him names and accused him of unnecessarily dividing the Southern Baptist Convention because he dared lead the way in race relations.

And Miss Kuhlman? Surely she had her critics also, even though I had not heard of any of them at the time. But I knew no woman could step out as she had without drawing the fire of many.

Why should I be different? Why should any follower of Christ run and hide just because those who refuse to accept the truth, those who cling to tradition rather than the Word of God, take up stones against them? I squeezed Ann's hand. I knew this: our lives had been touched by the power of the Holy Spirit. Whether that meant persecution—or praise—was immaterial. We could not deny what we had seen and heard.

The meeting was drawing to a close

when Miss Kuhlman suddenly raised one hand in the air. "We have witnessed the mercy of God in these blessings, but there is a far greater blessing for you if you are willing. Those who will accept Jesus Christ as personal Savior, those who want to be born again, get up from your seats and come to the front."

The aisles were filled with streams of people. They filled the platform, crowded around the base of the steps and back down the aisles. There was no more room, yet the people kept coming. Miss Kuhlman had to say, "Stand where you are. Make your commitment to Jesus as Savior and pray with me." It was a happy moment for us all, a fitting climax to a wonderful service.

Lance and Marshall returned the wheelchair to the car. I hoped I would never need it again. After the meeting we crossed the street to a Howard Johnson restaurant. It was crammed with people who had been at the Miracle Service. We talked with two nurses from the hospital in Alexandria until the restaurant closed. Both boys were asleep in the seats of the booth and we had to wake them to get them back to the car.

"Let's put this to the test," I said to Ann. "I'm going to drive home."

I had been able to drive short distances, but to sit in one position for any length of time, especially without my brace, had been impossible. It was a glorious night, though. The full moon was hanging still in the western sky, outlining the stately pines which stood like sentinels against the dark Louisiana horizon. I thought of that ride so many years ago when my life had been suddenly and drastically changed. Now it had been changed again. It was my hope, somehow, some way, through my testimony of the power of the Holy Spirit, I could reach out in a way I had never been able to reach out before. Perhaps that dream God placed in my heart as a young boy—that I could be a medical missionary—was not impossible. Perhaps I was to carry the word of the power of the Great Physician—through my healed body—in addition to setting broken bones and prescribing medicines and treatment. The boys were asleep in the back seat and Ann slipped over close to me. It had been twenty-one years since we'd ridden like that. I reached out and put my arm around her. It was as close to riding in heaven as I had ever been.

The next morning my son Brooks was in the kitchen fixing his breakfast before school when he heard me coming down the hall.

"It happened, didn't it?" he said, running to meet me.

"How did you know?" I asked, puzzled.

"It was the drag. I didn't hear you dragging your leg as you walked." He walked around me his eyes filled with amazement. "Wow! That's really something."

"Watch me kill a roach," I grinned, and stomped the floor hard with my "bad" leg.

Brooks' eyes grew even wider. "Wow! Wow!"

CHAPTER NINE

I Have Had No Pain in a Year!

I left for the office early that morning. There was something I wanted to do. The grass had grown high around the side of my office building. I brought a sickle from the house and went to work on it. I was out there swinging away when my two nurses arrived to open the office. They stood in the parking lot for a long time, looking. Then without a word they entered the building. When I finally came in, my face flushed from the exercise, they busied themselves, deliberately ignoring my strange behavior. They were yet to hear what had happened. Neither of them had ever seen me put weight on my leg in that way.

It was midmorning when I called Ann on the phone.

"Oh, Cliff, it's so wonderful. I've been reading everything I can find in the Bible about the Holy Spirit, miracles, and healings. The Holy Spirit has flooded me with love. It's like being baptized. I feel like a fool, but I'm walking around the house crying and laughing and telling God how much I love Him. I've never done that before, Cliff. I've never told God how much I love Him, but I can't stop. I'm shouting happy!"

She was like that for three days. Every time I came home she was happily praising God. And so was I. We couldn't sleep at night; there was such a glow in the bedroom. It was as though the entire house was wired with power. We talked, prayed, and praised God.

Something else was happening. That great inner peace which had settled in my spirit during the miracle service stayed with me. With it came a release from the fears and worries which had bothered me. At work I found I had received what can only be described as gifts from the Holy Spirit. Not only was I able to diagnose and prescribe treatment with a new ability, but I found I had a new spiritual insight into the needs of many of my patients.

Accompanying this was a strong feeling I should not "cast my pearls before swine." That meant I needed to be careful how and where I testified. Getting medical confirmation would take time. Even so, that was inconsequential since I had regained full use of my leg and the pain was totally gone. Besides, I didn't have to prove anything to anyone. All a person had to do was look at me and see I was different.

The next Wednesday night Ann and I attended the regular midweek prayer service at our church. At the church supper prior to the meeting I carried my own tray from the serving line to the table. The people watched. I just smiled and greeted them as usual. Like the nurses in my office, no one asked questions; they just looked.

Only our pastor, Dr. Houston Smith, commented. He saw me walking down the aisle after the service and missed the usual expression of pain on my face. I told him briefly what had taken place and he stood back, looking. "Wonderful! Praise God!" he exclaimed softly. "God is doing marvelous things. Nothing could surprise me."

It didn't take long for the word to get out that I was walking. The nurses in the hospital who were accustomed to my daily rounds in the wheelchair, my patients, other doctors, my friends, members of my church—all knew.

My mind was still fixed on the one method for treating medical information drilled into all medical students. There is no place for wishful thinking or subjective personal opinion.

Finally I called my doctor and made an appointment for my check-up. As usual, the x-rays were taken before he did anything else. The technician, who was the same person who made the x-rays just after the 1951 wreck, commented that he almost did not recognize me because something had changed drastically in my appearance. "Where are the pain lines you used to have in your face?" he asked.

As soon as the x-rays were developed I looked at them with my orthopedic board surgeon. "It's still the same, Cliff. You shouldn't put off the hip replacement much longer." The arthritic bony spurs of post-traumatic osteoarthritis of the joint were still there. The hip was still fused. By all rights I should be in excruciating pain. I wasn't.

Next was the physical examination check-up. He put me on the table and went through the various motions involving the hip as he controlled the motions with hands on my ankles. Passive and active ranges of motion were charted. The hip joint checked out with no pain or marked resistance to movement.

"I don't understand," he said. "If I get this kind of result with a total hip replace-ment, I am thrilled."

I dressed and we returned to his office. He looked at me with kindness and asked,

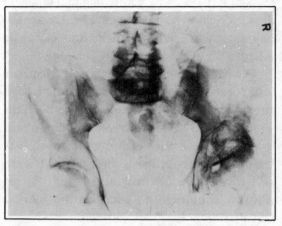

X-ray—osteoarthritis; right hip with fusion
and spur formation.

"How is your pain, Cliff?"

"I don't have any, Dan."

"You're lying."

"No, Dan, I am not lying. I have had
no pain in a year."

"You are still lying. We both know the
only way to get at that pain is by total hip
replacement."

"Have you heard of Kathryn Kuhlman?"

"No."

"Well, let me tell you a little about her." For the next few minutes I capsuled my experiences at the Miracle Service in Monroe. He listened attentively.

"The mind does have a lot of power over the body," was his comment.

My answer was, "I agree."

His waiting room was full of patients, so the remainder of the visit was brief. Dan made no attempt to hide the fact that he was happily surprised with his findings on the hip problem.

I thanked him and started down the hall towards the back parking lot. His nurse, who had been standing in the hall near the open door while we talked, hurried after me. "Dr. Harris, I want you to know that I watch the Kathryn Kuhlman telecast every Sunday. I think she is wonderful."

The fact that the constant pain and weakness were gone and that it was no problem to work long hours in comfort without the brace or wheelchair are the sort of things hard to put into words. Added to this, there was a heavenly peace which had come to me and has never left.

My life is still lived amidst the same circumstances and stress as ever. But the burden is lifted. I could not handle the problems anyway, so great were their demands. It is wonderful to release them all to God. Now they are His problems.

For years I have carefully avoided use of the word healing in reference to my condition. As a doctor I face too many different types of healing to ever treat healing as simple and easily defined. The x-rays of the right hip made in 1971 and those made in 1973 indicate that I should still be in pain. To use a more specific descriptive term, I prefer to say I have been made a whole person.

When Jesus approached the crippled man at the pool of Bethesda, He did not ask him if he wanted to be healed. Rather He asked, "Do you want to be made whole?"

To be healed in body is wonderful. To be made a whole person is better.

I have always been open to talk about Jesus with my patients, but now I often have the nurse pounding the bell from the treatment room to remind me others are waiting to be seen. I find I am far more prone to emphasize spiritual needs which pills will never touch. Every day brings new adventures.

CHAPTER TEN

I've Never Seen You Look So Well!

For quite some time I had been treating a retired service man for arthritis of the spine. He was a heavy-set patient, a former professional football player with the Detroit Lions. Even though he seldom talked, I found him very well read and a man of intelligence.

About two months after the Monroe meeting, in the course of his office visit, he asked me if I minded a personal question. "Why haven't you told me you were on television?" he asked.

"Not me," I replied.

Then he surprised me. "I saw you on

my own set on that stage with that lady. I
was thinking what a fake it was and suddenly, there you were and I saw you fall
down."

I was aware that television crews were
filming the service when I was talking to
Miss Kuhlman. I had even watched for it to
show on TV but finally decided it would
not be aired.

The Sunday following the meeting a full
hour was given on Channel 8 to show the
service and the claimed healings. Since it
was aired at 11:00 a.m. and I was attending
my own church service, I was unaware I
had missed it.

He continued, "I've been watching you
every visit here. You are not the same person. I have been waiting for you to mention
it, but you haven't. Will Kathryn Kuhlman
be back? Can I attend such a service?"

A few questions revealed that he had
grown up in a Greek Orthodox church
family. He was an avid reader of current
events as well as a wide range of books, but
the Bible was not one of them. He was out
of touch with evangelical Christianity. It

also came out that he was consuming a case of beer a day along with his medication to bear the pain.

In a most unexpected chain of events, while my mind was fixed on his search for physical healing, he had a life-shaking religious experience. He is an enthusiastic member of a nearby Southern Baptist church now. He teaches the young men's Bible class. He buys cassette sermons and Bible expositions from far and wide and makes copies to share with ministers and shut-in invalids who cannot attend church. He is still my patient and his radiance fills the office when he comes for his treatments. He is thrilled to give his testimony and adds that through his own obvious physical suffering, he believes that he comes across to the disabled in a special way.

In the summer of 1973, I was at the pediatrics nurses' station working on a chart. I glanced up to see my orthopedic surgeon standing nearby. I thought he had a patient and was getting a chart from the rack. He was intently watching me.

"How's your pain, Cliff?" he asked.

"Still don't have any, Dan. I really don't."

He shook his head. "I must admit I have never seen you look so well. You look great. Even the expression on your face is different. Now, who is that lady?" he asked.

"Kathryn Kuhlman," I replied.

"You are going to make a believer out of me yet," he remarked as he walked out.

At the time of Miss Kuhlman's death, I was in the office—it was a Saturday morning. The phone rang. It was Dan. I knew he would not be calling about a patient at that time. "Cliff, did you hear the news that Miss Kuhlman died last night?"

My reply was that I knew she was ill but had not heard more than that.

"This is a real loss to the world," he responded.

There is a common error that divine or miracle healing runs counter to scientific thinking. I have not found it a problem for doctors, whatever their religious thinking. It is seated prejudice built on information which is false, where we find "the rub."

Looking back, without being conscious it was even happening at the time, I can see how our fine medical school professors made the simple scientific truth about it clear to us. We were taught that all science relating to medicine reaches a boundary which is the capacity of the human mind to understand and that experiences which lie beyond that are simply not tackled by science because that would be unscientific. Religion was seldom touched in our lectures.

It was not strange to find that many of our professors faithfully attended church, had places of leadership in their churches and miracles were a vital part of their faith. On the other hand, we find Christians who, because of prejudice supported by ignorance and wrong opinions, still follow outdated positions on miracles.

Everywhere I go, among doctors, ministers, laymen alike, I am discovering there is a new and growing interest and acceptance of miracles, including those dealing with healing of the sick. It is far more than mind over matter. *It is the Lordship of the Creator over His creation!*

I could, being a doctor, go out and compile case histories of these dramatic healings. That would be Cliff Harris' approach. After all, what more evidence do I need than the evidence Ann and I live with? Here I am, a medical doctor, following a terrible car wreck, kept alive by brilliant scientist doctors like Dr. Rigsby Hargrove, going through major surgery performed by one of the finest orthopedic surgeons in the world, with my progress documented by credible medical evidence, including x-ray pictures of the degenerating, fusing, arthritic joint. Professionally competent where the prognosis is concerned, the specialists agreed that relief would be hopeless until successful total hip replacement surgery was done.

On the other hand, after an encounter with the power of the Holy Spirit of God: instant relief of pain, comfortable resumption of full hard schedule of medical practice, and not one day missed due to illness in the period doctors call the "five-year recovery rate."

What more can I say? What else is

necessary? Sometimes I am almost frightened when I stop to realize the responsibility that is mine and the confidence God has placed in me. Yet it is not my wisdom or might, but His that is the source of my life and strength, giving me power to witness and power for service. These are trying days for many and the burden often becomes very heavy, but I promise you that God is still on His throne and there is no need in life which the Lord cannot supply, no problem to which He does not hold the key. "Weeping may endure for a night, but joy cometh in the morning" in the sunshine of God's smile and matchless grace. We can depend on His mercy and the faithfulness of His Word, for He is our God and we are surrounded and guarded by His watchful love.

Epilogue

As to the question, "How is Dr. Harris now?" the letter quoted in part below will give you the answer. It was written by Dr. D. M. Kingsley on February 14, 1978, in response to an invitation he received to be a guest on nationwide television:

"The demands of my time are so great that I have to put off a great many things that I would like to do.

"Therefore, please excuse me from a personal appearance.

"Nevertheless, I will be glad to cooperate in any manner I can. I can testify to the fact that since Kathryn Kuhlman's contact with Dr. Harris, he has been a changed and new man. He strides around as if there is nothing wrong. His whole personality is changed for the better, and it is practically a miracle to see his improvement.

"From the medical standpoint, I have not been able to check his hip clinically nor with new x-rays, so I cannot say that there is any essential medical difference, but you are welcome to quote what I have said above."